HERCULES

D0535289

A Visit to
ENGLAND

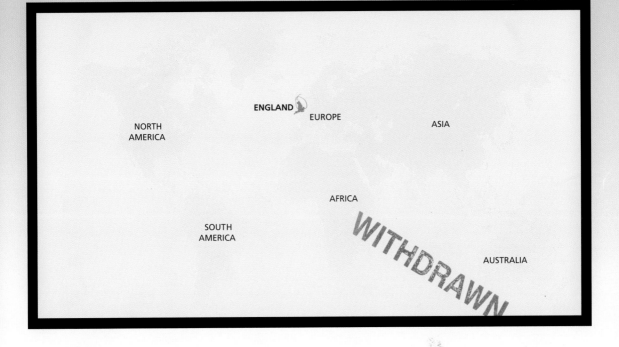

Chris Oxlade and Anita Ganeri

CONTRA COSTA COUNTY LIBRARY

3 1901 04062 9877

Heinemann Library
Chicago, Illinois

© 2003 Heinemann Library
a division of Reed Elsevier Inc.
Chicago, Illinois

Customer Service 888-454-2279
Visit our website at www.heinemannlibrary.com

All rights reserved. No part of this publication may be reproduced or transmitted in any form or by any means, electronic or mechanical, including photocopying, recording, taping, or any information storage and retrieval system, without permission in writing from the publisher.

Designed by Ron Kamen and StoreyBooks
Picture Research by Catherine Bevan and Ginny Stroud-Lewis
Originated by Dot Gradiations Ltd.
Printed in China by South China Printing Company

07 06 05 04
10 9 8 7 6 5 4 3 2

Library of Congress Cataloging-in-Publication Data
Ganeri, Anita, 1961-
  England / Anita Ganeri and Chris Oxlade.
     v. cm. -- (A visit to)
Includes bibliographical references and index.
Contents: England -- Land -- Landmarks -- Homes -- Food -- Clothes --Work -- Transportation -- Language -- School -- Free time -- Celebrations -- The arts -- Fact file -- Glossary -- More books to read.
  ISBN 1-40340-965-X (library binding-hardcover)
  1. England--Juvenile literature. [1. England.] I. Oxlade, Chris. II. Title. III. Series.
  DA27.5 .G36 2003
  942--dc21
                          2002007415

Acknowledgments
The author and publishers are grateful to the following for permission to reproduce copyright material: pp. 5, 6, 7, 8, 11, 12, 14, 15, 16, 17, 18, 21, 23, 24, 28, 29 Peter Evans; p. 9 Photodisc; p. 10 Trevor Clifford; p. 13 Collections/Roger Scruton; p. 19 Collections/Ray Roberts; p. 20 Corbis/Kim Sayer; p. 22 John Walmsley; p. 25 Collections/Paul Watts; p. 26 Collections/John Wender; p. 27 Trip/A. Tovy.
Cover photograph of Stonehenge, reproduced with permission of Photodisc.

Every effort has been made to contact copyright holders of any material reproduced in this book. Any omissions will be rectified in subsequent printings if notice is given to the publisher.

Some words are shown in bold, **like this.** You can find out what they mean by looking in the glossary.

Contents

England

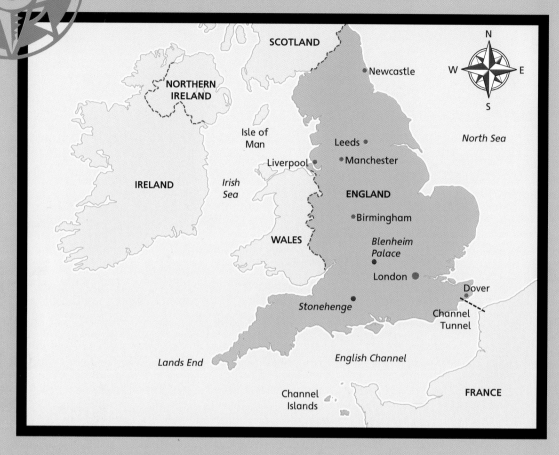

England is a country in the United Kingdom. It is also part of a group of islands called the British Isles. About 50 million people live in England.

The **capital** city of England is called London. It is built along the Thames River. The buildings on the right side of the river are the **Houses of Parliament**.

Land

Most of the land in England is very flat. It is divided up into fields with **hedges** between them. Farmers raise animals or grow crops in the fields.

England has a long **coastline**. In the
south and west, the coastline can be
rocky, with steep cliffs. The east coast
is often flat, and has beaches.

Landmarks

This is Blenheim Palace in central England. There are many **stately homes** like this in the English countryside. You can visit many of them and look around inside.

This circle of stones is called Stonehenge. People began building Stonehenge many years ago, dragging each stone into place. They may have used the stones to **worship** the Sun.

Homes

Most English people live in towns and cities. Some live in streets of **semi-detached** houses like these. Many families own their own homes instead of **renting** them.

In most towns in England, there are streets of houses joined together in long rows. They are called **terraced** houses. Many of these have a small backyard.

Food

This is a **traditional** English breakfast. It has bacon, sausages, tomatoes, mushrooms, eggs, fried bread, and baked beans. Not many people eat like this every day!

There are many restaurants in England that serve food from other countries of the world. Indian dishes, such as **curries** and spicy pickles, are very popular here.

13

Clothes

When they are relaxing at home
or out playing with their friends,
young people in England wear clothes
like T-shirts, jeans, and sportswear.

Most children wear a **uniform** when they are at school. In some schools, children must wear jackets and ties, like the boys here. In other schools, the uniform is less formal.

Work

Millions of people in England travel to a town or city every day to work. Some drive a car or ride a bike. Many more travel by bus or train.

Many people from other countries visit
England every year. Many English people
work in jobs that have something to do
with **tourism**.

Transportation

Buses, **trams,** and underground trains carry people around England's city centers. This is the main bus station in Liverpool. All the city buses start and finish their journeys here.

This train carries people between London, France, and Belgium. It runs under the sea in a tunnel between England and France.

Language

Most people in England speak English. In different parts of the country, people speak with different **accents**. People in some areas even have their own words for things.

Many people move to England from other countries. They speak languages other than English. Newsstands in England sell newspapers written in different languages.

School

In England, children start school when they are four or five years old. They must go to school until they are sixteen years old. This is a **primary school** classroom.

These children go to a primary school in a country village. When they are eleven years old, they will travel to a larger school in the nearest town.

Free Time

In England, children enjoy playing and watching sports such as **cricket, football,** tennis, and **netball**. Cricket, tennis, and football were first played in England.

People enjoy **sightseeing** on the weekends and during school vacations. There are many **stately homes**, pretty beaches, and beautiful parts of the country to visit.

Celebrations

A man named Guy Fawkes tried to blow up the **Houses of Parliament** on November 5, 1605. People light bonfires and set off fireworks to celebrate Guy Fawkes Night.

The Notting Hill Carnival takes place in
August. People dress up in costumes
and parade through Notting Hill, a
part of London.

The Arts

England has many art galleries. They show paintings, **sculptures,** and other works of art. This gallery in Liverpool has paintings by many famous artists.

England has many theaters. This is the Globe Theatre in London. It is a copy of the theater where William Shakespeare's plays were first performed many years ago.

Fact File

Name	England is part of the United Kingdom of Great Britain and Northern Ireland.
Capital	The **capital** city is London.
Language	English is the official language of England.
Population	About 50 million people live in England.
Money	Money is called pounds sterling. Its symbol is £.
Religion	The official Christian church in England is called the Church of England. There are several other churches, too. There are also many Muslims, Jews, Hindus, and Sikhs in England.
Products	England produces medicines, fibers and textiles, electronics, cars, parts for planes, household goods, and fruits, vegetables, and animals for food. Finance and **tourism** are also important.

Words you can learn

North East (Geordie)	tatie	potato
	why-aye	of course
London (cockney rhyming slang)	pen and ink	stink
	mince pies	eyes
Midlands	fizzog	face
	mardy	grumpy
Cornwall (Cornish)	ha sos	hello
	dew genough	goodbye
Yorkshire	ey up	hello
	flibberty gibbet	person who talks too much

Glossary

accent	way words sound when people say them
capital	most important city
coastline	where the edge of the land meets the sea
cricket	English game similar to American baseball
curries	Indian dishes flavored with herbs and spices
football	English word for the American game of soccer
hedge	line of bushes around a field
Houses of Parliament	buildings containing the two groups that make up the United Kingdom government
netball	team game based on running, jumping, throwing, and catching
primary school	school for children between five and eleven years old
renting	paying to live in someone else's house
sculpture	work of art shaped out of wood, stone or other things
semi-detached	house that is joined to another on one side only
sightseeing	visiting interesting or beautiful places
stately homes	large houses surrounded by parks and gardens
terraced	houses that are joined together in a row
tourism	business to do with people visiting places on trips or vacations
traditional	something that has been done the same way for many years
tram	vehicle on rails used to transport passengers on city streets
uniform	clothes that people have to wear so they all look the same
worship	praising and saying prayers to something or someone

Index

More Books to Read

Burgan, Michael. *England*. New York: Scholastic Library Publishing, 1999.

Davis, Kevin A. *Look What Came from England*. New York: Scholastic Library Publishing, 2000.

Schemenauer, Elma. *England*. Eden Prairie, Minn.: The Child's World, Incorporated, 2000.

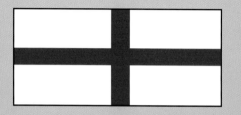

The St George's Cross is the flag of England.